VENICE PRESERVED.

A Tragedy

·N FIVE ACTS

BY THOMAS OTWAY.

WITH THE STAGE BUSINESS, CAST OF CHARACTERS, COS-
TUMES, RELATIVE POSITIONS, &c.

—

1874.

EDITORIAL INTRODUCTION.

THE story of " Venice Preserved" is partly founded upon St.
Real's History of the Conspiracy of the Spaniards against the
Republic of Venice, in 1618. Voltaire compares the author of
this History to Sallust; and pronounces it superior to the English tragedy—an assertion, which, like many others from the
same source, was the convenient sentence of an adroit but reck-
less ignorance. The merits of St. Real are undoubtedl·· great ;
but Otway's indebtedness to him is exceedingly slight ; and it is
rt markable to see how ingeniously, from a few meagre historical
details, the great dramatist has constructed one of the noblest
imaginative works of which literature can boast. The *names* of
nearly all the *dramatis personæ*, with the exception of *Belvidera*,
are taken from St. Real ; but their *characters* are Otway's, and
his plot is almost wholly original. The true *Pierre* was a Nor-
man corsair, who had accumulated a fortune by plundering ships
in the Mediterranean. He was eventually strangled on board
his own ship by order of the Venetian Senate. *Jaffier* was of
Provence, and appears to have engaged in the plot against the
state from his friendship for Pierre, and the prospect of gain.
History says nothing of his wrongs, or his love for the daughter
of *Priuli ;* and he was shaken in his faith to the conspiracy, not
by the tears of a woman, but partly by his detestation of the
sanguinary speech of *Renault* (in which Otway follows the
history), and partly from being struck with compunction during
the spectacle of the Doge's wedding the Adriatic, when his ima-
gination contrasted the public rejoicings with the desolation which
was to follow. After disclosing the plot, and experiencing the
perfidy of the Senate, who had promised him the lives of his
friends, he was made captive while bearing arms against Venice,

and drowned the day after his arrival in the city. *Renault,* ac
cording to St. Real, was an old French gentleman, who had fled
to Venice for some unknown cause, and there became acquainteo
with the *Marquis de Bedmar.* Though poor, he esteemed virtue more than riches, and glory more than virtue. He had abi-
lities, courage, a contempt for life, and a passion for distinction.
The affront towards Belvidera, of which Otway makes him
guilty, was a pure invention of the author, unsupported by any
trait which history ascribes to Renault.

Few plays owe so much to the pruning-knife for their success
as this. In its unexpurgated state, "Venice Preserved" leaves
an impression far less favorable to the genius, as well as the
moral sense of the author, than in its present abridged and recti-
fied shape. In the language of Campbell, " never were beauties
and faults more easily separated than those of this tragedy. The
latter, in its purification for the stage, came off like dirt from a
fine statue, taking away nothing from its symmetrical surface,
and leaving us only to wonder how the author himself should
have soiled it with such disfigurements. *Pierre* is a miserable
conspirator, as Otway first painted him, impelled to treason by
his love of a courtesan and his jealousy of *Antonio.* But his character, as it now comes forward, is a mixture of patriotism and
excusable misanthropy. Even in the more modern prompt-
books, an improving curtailment has been introduced. Until the
middle of the last century, the ghosts of *Jaffier* and *Pierre* used
to come in upon the stage, haunting *Belvidera* in her last agonies,
which, Heaven knows, require no aggravation from spectral
agency."

This tragedy is believed to have been originally acted about
the year 1682. " *Pierre* and *Jaffier,*" says Jackson, in his History of the Scottish Stage, " in the estimation of the theatrical
world, are equal in rank, and excel each other in representation
only, as the particular talents of the actor elevate or lessen, in
the idea of the spectator, the importance of whichever part he
assumes. I have seen Garrick and Barry alternately in both
parts, and the candid critic was doubtful where to bestow the
preference. Mr. Mossop, indeed, raised the character of *Pierre*
beyond all reach, and left any *Jaffier* I ever saw with him at a

distance; but, had he attempted *Jaffier*, I am confident he would, with Barry in *Pierre*, have stood far behind."

Of this same Mossop in *Pierre*, Davies, the biographer of Garrick, remarks :—

"His fine, full-toned voice and strong expression of sentiment, gave uncommon spirit to the warmth and passion of the character. In the interview with the conspirators, in the third act, he threw a gallantry into his action, as striking as it was unexpected. But he greatly excelled in the vehement reproaches, which, in the fourth act, he poured, with acrimony and force, on the treachery and cowardice of Jaffier. The cadences of his voice were equally adapted to the loudest rage and the most deep and solemn reflection, which he judiciously varied."

"Mr. Garrick," says Davies, "when fixed in the management of Drury Lane, resigned *Pierre*, in which part his fire and spirit were not equally supported by grandeur and dignity of person, for *Jaffier*, which he acted with great and deserved approbation many years. The temporary frenzy, with which *Jaffier* is seized, in the fourth act, on fancying that he saw his friend on the rack, has not since been equalled, nor, perhaps, ever will:

——' He groans;
Hark, how he groans! his screams are in my ears
Already! See, they've fixed him on the wheel!
And now they tear him! Murder! Perjured Senate!
Murder !'

"The enthusiastic power of Garrick presented this dreadful image to the audience with such astonishing force, that they trembled at the imaginary picture. In all the softer scenes of domestic woe, conjugal tenderness, and agonizing distress, Barry, it must be owned, was Garrick's master.

"Mrs. Cibber was long the *Belvidera* of Barry and Garrick. Every situation seemed to be formed on purpose to call forth her great skill in awakening the passions. Mrs. Siddons has, in this part as well as many others, fixed the favor of the town in her behalf. This actress, like a resistless torrent, has borne down all before her. In person, just rising above the middle stature, she looks, walks, and moves, like a woman of superior rank. Her countenance is expressive; her eye so full of information, that the passion is told from her look before she speaks. Her voice, though not so harmonious as Mrs. Cibber's, is strong and pleasing: nor is a word lost for want of due articulation. She excels all performers in paying due attention to the business of the scene. Her eye never wanders from the person she speaks to, or should look at when she is silent. Her modulation of grief, in her plaintive pronunciation of the interjection, Oh! is sweetly moving, and reaches to the heart. Her madness in Belvidera is terribly affecting. The many accidents of spectators falling into fainting-fits during her acting, bear testimony to the effects of her exertions. She certainly does not spare herself. None can say that she is not in *downright earnest*.'

Thomas Otway, the author of this and some nine other plays, of various merit, none of which, however, now keep possession of the stage, was the son of a clergyman, and born at Trotting in Sussex, England, in the year 1651. His tragedy of the " Orphan" was for many years as attractive in the representation as " Venice Preserved ;" but the plot is of a character to render it distasteful to a modern audience, although it contains passages of remarkable beauty and power. Otway is said to have tried his fortune on the stage as an actor, and to have failed—not an unfrequent case with dramatic authors. He appears to have earned but a precarious subsistence by his pen; although from the little we can glean of his history, the inference is, he was improvident, and easily led away by gay, dissipated companions. One of his biographers gives a melancholy account of the destitution of his latter days, and states, that he was reduced to the necessity of borrowing a shilling, to satisfy the cravings of hunger, from a gentleman, who, shocked at the distress of the author of " Venice Preserved," put a guinea into his hands; that Otway was choked with a piece of bread, which he had immediately purchased. He is said to have died the 14th April, 1685. at a public-house on Tower Hill. This story is contradicted by Dr. Warton, who says that the poet died of a distemper brought on by a severe cold.

Out of Shakspeare's unapproachable domain, we know of no tragedy in the English language to compare with this in the earnestness of its passion, the depth of its pathos, and the aptitude of its language. Although it has not been represented of late years as frequently as formerly, it will be long before it is superseded in its foremost rank in our acting drama.

VENICE PRESERVED

· ACT 1.

SCENE I.—*St. Mark's.*

Enter PRIULI *and* JAFFIER, L.

Priuli. (R.) No more! I'll hear no more! Begone
and leave me!
Jaf. Not hear me! By my sufferings, but you shall!
My lord—my lord! I'm not that abject wretch
You think me. Patience! where's the distance throws
Me back so far, but I may boldly speak
In right, though proud oppression will not hear me?
Priuli. Have you not wronged me?
Jaf. Could my nature e'er
Have brooked injustice, or the doing wrongs,
I need not now thus low have bent myself
To gain a hearing from a cruel father.—
Wronged you?
Priuli. Yes, wronged me! In the nicest point,
The honour of my house, you've done me wrong.
You may remember (for I now will speak,
And urge its baseness) when you first came home
From travel, with such hopes as made you looked on
By all men's eyes, a youth of expectation;
Pleased with your growing virtue, I received you;
Courted, and sought to raise you to your merits;
My house, my table, nay, my fortune too,
My very self was yours; you might have used me
To your best service; like an open friend,

I treated, trusted you, and thought you mine :
When, in requital of my best endeavours,
You treacherously practised to undo me ;
Seduced the weakness of my age's darling,
My only child, and stole her from my bosom.
Oh ! Belvidera !

    Jaf. 'Tis to me you owe her :
Childless you had been else, and in the grave
Your name extinct ; no more Priuli heard of.
You may remember, scarce five years are past,
Since in your brigantine you sailed to see
The Adriatic wedded by our duke ;
And I was with you : your unskilful pilot
Dashed us upon a rock ; when to your boat
You made for safety ; entered first yourself ;—
Th' affrighted Belvidera, following next,
As she stood trembling on the vessel's side,
Was, by a wave, washed off into the deep ;
When instantly I plunged into the sea,
And buffeting the billows to her rescue,
Redeemed her life with half the loss of mine.
Like a rich conquest, in one hand I bore her,
And with the other dashed the saucy waves,
That thronged and pressed to rob me of my prize.
I brought her, gave her to your despairing arms ;
Indeed, you thanked me ; but a nobler gratitude
Rose in her soul : for from that hour she loved me,
Till for her life she paid me with herself.

    Priuli. You stole her from me ; like a thief you stole
      her,
At dead of night ; that cursèd hour you chose
To rifle me of all my heart held dear.
May all your joys in her prove false, like mine !
A sterile fortune, and a barren bed,
Attend you both : continual discord make
Your days and nights bitter and grievous still :
May the hard hand of a vexatious need
Oppress and grind you ; till at last you find
The curse of disobedience all your portion.

    Jaf. Half of your curse you have bestowed in vain.
Heav'n has already crowned our faithful loves
With a young boy, sweet as his mother's beauty :

May he live to prove more gentle than his grandsire,
And happier than his father.
Priuli. Rather live
To bait thee for his bread, and din your ears
With hungry cries; whilst his unhappy mother
Sits down and weeps in bitterness of want.
    Jaf. You talk as if 'twould please you.
    Priuli. 'Twould, by heaven!
    Jaf. Would I were in my grave!
    Priuli. And she, too, with thee:
For, living here, you're but my cursed remembrancers,
I once was happy!
    Jaf. You use me thus, because you know my soul
Is fond of Belvidera. You perceive
My life feeds on her, therefore thus you treat me
Were I that thief, the doer of such wrongs
As you upbraid me with, what hinders me
But I might send her back to you with contumely,
And court my fortune where she would be kinder?
    Priuli. You dare not do't.
    Jaf. Indeed, my lord, I dare not.
My heart, that awes me, is too much my master:
Three years are past since first our vows were plighted,
During which time, the world must bear me witness,
I've treated Belvidera like your daughter,
The daughter of a senator of Venice:
Distinction, place, attendance, and observance,
Due to her birth, she always has commanded:
Out of my little fortune, I've done this;
Because, (though hopeless e'er to win your nature)
The world might see I loved her for herself;
Not as the heiress of the great Priuli.
    Priuli. No more.
    Jaf. Yes, all, and then, adieu forever.
       [*Pausing with clasped hands*
There's not a wretch that lives on common charity
But's happier than I; for I have known
The luscious sweets of plenty; every night
Have slept with soft content about my head,
And never waked, but to a joyful morning:
Yet now must fall, like a full ear of corn,
Whose blossom 'scaped, yet's withered in the ripening

Priuli. Home, and be humble; study to ret: ench;
Discharge the lazy vermin of thy hall,
Those pageants of thy folly:
Reduce the glitt'ring trappings of thy wife
To humble weeds, fit for thy little state :   '*Going,* ·
Then to some suburb cottage both retire ;
Drudge to feed loathsome life ; get brats and starve—
Home, home, I say !   [*Exit,* R.
    Jaf. (c.) Yes, if my heart would let me——
This proud, this swelling heart : home I would go,
But that my doors are hateful to my eyes,
Filled and damned up with gaping creditors !
I've now not fifty ducats in the world,
Yet still I am in love, and pleased with ruin.
Oh, Belvidera ! Oh ! she is my wife—
And we will bear our wayward fate together,
But ne'er know comfort more.

                Enter PIERRE, L. S. E.

    Pierre. (L. C.) My friend, good morrow;
How fares the honest partner of my heart ?
What, melancholy ! not a word to spare me!
    Jaf. (c.) I'm thinking, Pierre, how that damned star-
        ing quality,
Called honesty, got footing in the world.
    Pierre. Why, powerful villainy first set it up,
For its own ease and safety. Honest men
Are the soft easy cushions on which knaves
Repose and fatten. Were all mankind villains,
They'd starve each other ; lawyers would want practice,
Cut-throats, reward : each man would kill his brother
Himself ; none would be paid or hanged for murder.
Honesty ! 'twas a cheat, invented first
To bind the hands of bold deserving rogues,
That fools and cowards might sit safe in power,
And lord it uncontrolled above their betters.
    Jaf. Then honesty is but a notion ?
    Pierre. Nothing else ;
Like wit, much talked of, not to be defined :
He that pretends to most, too, has least share in't.
Tis a ragged virtue. Honesty ! no more on't.
    Jaf. Sure, thou art honest ?

Pierre. So, indeed, men think me;
But they're mistaken, Jaffier; I'm a rogue,
As well as they;
A fine, gay, bold-faced villain as thou seest me!
'Tis true, I pay my debts, when they're contracted;
I steal from no man; would not cut a throat
To gain admission to a great man's purse;
Would not betray my friend,
To get his place or fortune; I scorn to flatter
A blown-up fool above me, or crush the wretch beneath
    me;
Yet, Jaffier, for all this, I am a villain.
    Jaf. (R. C.) A villain!
    Pierre. Yes, a most notorious villain;
To see the sufferings of my fellow-creatures,
And own myself a man; to see our senators
Cheat the deluded people with a show
Of liberty, which yet they ne'er must taste of.
They say, by them our hands are free from fetters;
Yet whom they please, they lay in basest bonds;
Bring whom they please to infamy and sorrow;
Drive us, like wrecks, down the rough tide of power,
Whilst no hold's left to save us from destruction.
All that bear this are villains, and I one,
Not to rouse up at the great call of nature,
And check the growth of these domestic spoilers,
That make us slaves, and tell us 'tis our charter!
                              [*Walks,* L.
    Jaf. I think no safety can be here for virtue,
And grieve, my friend, as much as thou, to live
In such a wretched state as this of Venice,
Where all agree to spoil the public good,
And villains fatten with the brave man's labours.
    Pierre. [*Returns to* L. C.) We've neither safety, unity,
        nor peace,
For the foundation's lost of common good;
Justice is lame, as well as blind, amongst us;
The laws (corrupted to their ends that make them,)
Serve but for instruments of some new tyranny,
That every day starts up, t'enslave us deeper.
Now [*Lays his hand on Jaffier's arm,*] could this glorious
    cause but find out friends

To dc it right, oh, Jaffier! then might'st thou
Not wear those seals of woe upon thy face;
The proud Priuli should be taught humanity,
And learn to value such a son as thou art.
I dare not speak, but my heart bleeds this moment.
　Jaf. Cursed be the cause, though I, thy friend, be part
　　on't:
Let me partake the troubles of thy bosom,
For I am used to misery, and perhaps
May find a way to sweeten't to thy spirit.
　Pierre. [*Turns, L. and looks over R. shoulder.*] Too soon
　·　'twill reach thy knowledge—
　Jaf. Then from thee
Let it proceed. There's virtue in thy friendship,
Would make the saddest tale of sorrow pleasing,
Strengthen my constancy, and welcome ruin.
　Pierre. Then thou art ruined!
　Jaf. That I long since knew;
I and ill fortune have been long acquainted.
　Pierre. I passed this very moment by thy doors,
And found them guarded by a troop of villains;
" The sons of public rapine were destroying."
They told me, by the sentence of the law
They had commission to seize all thy fortune:
Nay, more, Priuli's cruel hand had signed it.
Here stood a ruffian, with a horrid face,
Lording it o'er a pile of massy plate,
Tumbled into a heap for public sale:
There was another making villainous jests
At thy undoing: he had ta'en possession
Of all thy ancient, most domestic ornaments;
Rich hangings, intermixed and wrought with gold
The very bed, which, on thy wedding night,
Received thee to the arms of Belvidera,
The scene of all thy joys, was violated
By the coarse hands of filthy dungeon villains,
And thrown amongst the common lumber
　Jaf. Now, thank heaven—
　Pierre. Thank heaven! for what?
　Jaf. That I'm not worth a ducat.
　Pierre. Curse thy dull stars, and the worse fate of Ve-
　　nice,

Where brothers, friends, and fathers, all are false ;
Where there's no truth, no trust; where innocence
Stoops under vile oppression, and vice lords it.
Hadst thou but seen, as I did, how, at last,
Thy beauteous Belvidera, like a wretch
That's doomed to banishment, came weeping forth,
Whilst two young virgins, on whose arms she leaned,
Kindly looked up, and at her grief grew sad,
As if they catched the sorrows that fell from her :
Ev'n the lewd rabble, that were gathered round
To see the sight, stood mute when they beheld her ;
Governed their roaring throats, and grumbled pity :
I could have hugged the greasy rogues ; they pleased me.
  Jaf. I thank thee for this story, from my soul ;
Since now I know the worst that can befall me.
Ah, Pierre ! I have a heart that could have borne
The roughest wrong my fortune could have done me ;
But when I think what Belvidera feels,
The bitterness her tender spirits taste of,
I own myself a coward. Bear my weakness,
If, throwing thus my arms about thy neck,   [*Embrace.*
I play the boy, and blubber in thy bosom.
Oh, I shall drown thee with my sorrows.
  Pierre. Burn,
First, burn and level Venice to thy ruin.
What ! starve, like beggars' brats, in frosty weather,
Under a hedge, and whine ourselves to death !
Thou, or thy cause, shall never want assistance,
Whilst I have blood or fortune fit to serve thee :
Command my heart, thour't every way its master.
  Jaf. No ; there's a secret pride in bravely dying.
  Pierre. Rats die in holes and corners, dogs run mad
Man knows a braver remedy for sorrow—.
Revenge, the attribute of gods ; they stamped it,
With their great image, on our natures. Die !
Consider well the cause that calls upon thee ,
And, if thou'rt base enough, die then. Remember
Thy Belvidera suffers ; Belvidera !
Die !—damn first !—What ! be decently interred
In a.church-yard, and mingle thy brave dust
With stinking rogues, that rot in winding-sheets,
Surfeit-slain fools, the common dung o'th' soil !

Jaf. On —
Pierre. Well said, out with't—swear a little—
Jaf. Swear! By sea and air; by earth, by hear'n and
hell,
I will revenge my Belvidera's tears!   [*Both go to the* R.
Hark thee, my friend—Priuli—is—a senator!
Pierre. A dog!
Jaf. Agreed.   [*Return to* c.
Pierre. Shoot him!
Jaf. With all my heart!
No more—where shall we meet at night?
Pierre. I'll tell thee:
On the Rialto, every night at twelve,
I take my evening's walk of meditation:
There we two'll meet, and talk of precious mischief.
Jaf. Farewell!
Pierre. At twelve.
Jaf. At any hour: my plagues
Will keep me waking.   [*Exit Pierre,* R.
(R. c.) Tell me why, good Heaven,
Thou mad'st me what I am, with all the spirit,
Aspiring thoughts, and elegant desires,
That fill the happiest man? Ah, rather, why
Didst thou not form me sordid as my fate,
Base-minded, dull, and fit to carry burdens?
Why have I sense to know the curse that's on me?
Is this just dealing, nature? Belvidera!
Poor Belvidera!
Bel. [*Without.*] Lead me, lead me, my virgins,
To that kind voice.

Enter BELVIDERA, L.

My lord, my love, my refuge!   [*Leans on Jaffier,* R. c
Happy my eyes when they behold thy face!
My heavy heart will leave its doleful beating
At sight of thee, and bound with sprightful joys.
Oh, smile! as when our loves were in their spring,
And cheer my fainting soul!
Jaf. (R. c.) As when our loves
Were in their spring! Has, then, my fortune changed
thee?
Art thou not, Belvidera, still the same,

Kind, good, and tender, as my arms first found thee ?
If thou art altered, where shall I have harbour ?
Where ease my loaded heart ? [*Part.*] Oh ! where ccm-
    plain ?
    Bel. (c.) Does this appear like change, or love decaying,
When thus I throw myself into thy bosom,
With all the resolution of strong truth !
                            [*Leans on Jaffier, R. c.*
I joy more in thee
Than did thy mother, when she hugged thee first,
And blessed the gods for all her travail past.
    Jaf. Can there in woman be such glorious faith ?
Sure, all ill stories of thy sex are false !   [*Part.*
Oh, woman ! lovely woman ! Nature made thee
To temper man : we had been brutes without you !
Angels are painted fair to look like you :
There's in you all that we believe of heaven ;
Amazing brightness, purity, and truth,
Eternal joy, and everlasting love !   [*Embrace.*
    Bel. If love be treasure, we'll be wondrous rich ;
Oh ! lead me to some desert, [*Part,*] wide and wild,
Barren as our misfortunes, where my soul
May have its vent, where I may tell aloud
To the high heavens, and ev'ry list'ning planet,
With what a boundless stock my bosom's fraught.
    Jaf. [*Taking her hand.*] Oh, Belvidera ! doubly I'm a
        beggar ;
Undone by fortune, and in debt to thee.
Want, worldly want, that hungry meagre fiend,
Is at my heels, and chases me in view.
Canst thou bear cold and hunger ? Can these limbs,
Framed for the tender offices of love,
Endure the bitter gripes of smarting poverty ?
When banished by our miseries abroad,
(As suddenly we shall be) to seek out,
In some far climate, where our names are strangers,
For charitable succour ; wilt thou then,
When in a bed of straw we shrink together,
Anp the bleak winds shall whistle round our heads ;
Wilt thou then talk thus to me ? Wilt thou then
Hush my cares thus, and shelter me with love ?
    Bel. Oh ! I will love thee, even in madness love thee !

Though my distracted senses should forsake me,
I'd find some intervals when my poor heart
Should 'suage itself, and be let loose to thine.
Though the bare earth be all our resting place,
Its roots our food, some cliff our habitation,
I'll make this arm a pillow for thine head;
And, as thou sighing liest, and swelled with sorrow,
Creep to thy bosom, pour the balm of love
Into thy soul, and kiss thee to thy rest ;   [Part.
Then praise our God, and watch thee till the morning.
    Jaf. Hear this, you Heav'ns, and wonder how you made
        her !
Reign, reign, ye monarchs, that divide the world ;
Busy rebellion ne'er will let you know
Tranquillity and happiness like mine ;
Like gaudy ships, the obsequious billows fall,
And rise again, to lift you in your pride ;
They wait but for a storm, and then devour you :
                        [Belvidera crosses, it
I, in my private bark already wrecked,
Like a poor merchant, driven to unknown land,
That had, by chance, picked up his choicest treasure,
In one dear casket, and saved only that;
                        [Returns to Jaffier
Since I must wander farther on the shore,
Thus [Taking her arm,] hug my little, but my precious
        store,
Resolved to scorn, and trust my fate no more. [Exeun', t

        END OF ACT I.

        ACT II.

        SCENE I.—The Rialto.

        Enter JAFFIER, L.

    Jaf. (L. C.) I'm here; and thus, the shades of night
        around me,
I look as if all hell were in my heart,

Ani I in hell. Nay, surely 'tis so with me!—
For every step I tread, methinks some fiend
Knocks at my breast, and bids me not be quiet.
I've heard how desperate wretches like myself,
Have wandered out at this dead time of night,
To meet the foe of mankind in his walk.
Sure I'm so cursed, that, though of Heav'n forsaken,
No minister of darkness cares to tempt me.
Hell! hell! why sleep'st thou ?   [*Turns, L.*

Enter PIERRE, R. S. E.

Pierre. Sure I've staid too long :   [*Coming forward.*
The clock has struck, and I may lose my proselyte.
Speak, [*Seeing Jaffier,*] who goes there ?
Jaf. (L.) A dog, that comes to howl
At yonder moon.   What's he, that asks the question ;
Pierre. A friend to dogs, for they are honest creatures,
And ne'er betray their masters ; never fawn
On any that they love not.   Well met, friend. [*Advancing
        toward,* R. C.] Jaffier !
Jaf. The same.
Pierre. (R. C.) Where's Belvidera ?
Jaf. For a day or two,
I've lodged her privately, till I see farther
What fortune will do with me.   Pry'thee, friend,
If thou wouldst have me fit to hear good counsel,
Speak not of Belvidera——
Pierre. (C.) Speak not of her ?
Jaf. Oh, no! nor name her ?
Pierre. May be, I wish her well.
Jaf. Whom well ?
Pierre. Thy wife; thy lovely Belvidera !
I hope a man may wish his friend's wife well,
And no harm done ?
Jaf. [*Retiring,* L.] You're merry, Pierre.
Pierre. [*Following.*] I am so :
Thou shalt smile, too, and Belvidera smile :
We'll all rejoice.   Here's something to buy pins ;
Marriage is chargeable.   [*Gives him a purse.*
   Jaf. (L.) I but half wished
To see the devil, and he's here already !   Well !
What must this buy ?   Rebellion, murder, treason ?

Tell me [*Turning* R.] which way I must bo damned for
  this.
  Pierre. (L. C.) When last we parted, we'd no qualms
  like these,
But entertained each other's thoughts, like men
Whose souls were well acquainted. Is the world
Reformed since our last meeting? What new miracles
Have happened? Has Priuli's heart relented?
Can he be honest?
  Jaf. Kind Heaven, let heavy curses
Gall his old age, till life become his burden;
Let him groan under't long, linger an age
In the worst agonies and pangs of death
And find its ease, but late!
  Pierre. Nay, couldst thou not
As well, my friend, have stretched the curse to all
The senate round, as to one single villain?
  Jaf, But curses stick not; could I kill with cursing,
By Heaven, I know not thirty heads in Venice
Should not be blasted! Senators should rot,
Like dogs, on dunghills. Oh, for a curse
To kill with!   [*Crosses*, R.
  Pierre. Daggers, daggers are much better.
  Jaf. (R. C.) Ha!
  Pierre. Daggers.
  Jaf. But where are they?
  Pierre. Oh! a thousand
May be disposed, in honest hands, in Venice.
  Jaf. Thou talk'st in clouds.
  Pierre. But yet a heart, half wronged
As thine has been, would find the meaning, Jaffier!
  Jaf. A thousand daggers, all in honest hands!
And have not I a friend will stick one here?
  Pierre. (C.) Yes, if I thought thou wert not to be che-
    rished
To a nobler purpose, I would be that friend:
                          [*Lays his hand on Jaffier's arm*
But thou hast better friends; friends, whom thy wrongs
Have made thy friends; friends, worthy to be called so.
I'll trust thee with a secret. There are spi ts
This Lour at work. But, as thou art a man,
Whom I have picked and chosen from the world,

Swear that thou wilt be true to what I utter;
And when I've told thee that, which only gods,
And men like gods, are privy to, then swear,
No chance, or change, shall wrest it from thy bosom
    Jaf. (R.) When thou wouldst bind me, is there need of
        oaths?
'Is coward, fool, or villain, in my face?
If I seem none of these, I dare believe
Thou wouldst not use me in a little cause;
For I am fit for honour's toughest task,
Nor ever yet found fooling was my province:
And, for a villainous, inglorious enterprize,
I know thy heart so well, I dare lay mine
Before thee, set it to what point thou wilt.
    Pierre. Nay, 'tis a cause thou wilt be fond of, Jaffier
For it is founded on the noblest basis;
Our liberties, our natural inheritance!
We'll do the business, and ne'er fast and pray for't;
Openly act a deed, the world shall gaze
With wonder at, and envy when 'tis done.
    Jaf. For liberty!
    Pierre. For liberty, my friend.   [*Jaffier crosses,* L.
Thou shalt be freed from base Priuli's tyranny,
And thy sequestered fortunes healed again;
I shall be free from those opprobrious wrongs
That press me now, and bend my spirit downward;
All Venice free, and every growing merit
Succeed to its just right; fools shall be pulled
From wisdom's seat; those baleful unclean birds,
Those lazy owls, who, perched near fortune's top,
Sit only watchful with their heavy wings
To cuff down new-fledged virtues, that would rise
To nobler heights, and make the grove harmonious.
    Jaf. What can I do?   [*Crosses to* R. D
    Pierre. Canst thou not kill a senator?
    Jaf. By all my wrongs, thou talk'st as if revenge
Were to be had! and the brave story warms me.
                                        [*Crosses,* L
    Pierre. Swear, then!
    Jaf. I do, [*Kneels.* L. C.] by all those glittering stars,
And yon great ruling planet of the night!
By all good spirits above, and ill below!

By love and friendship, dearer than my life,
No powcr, nor death, shall make me false to thee !
 Pierre. Here we embrace, and I'll unlock my heart.
A council's held hard by, where the destruction
Of this great empire's hatching ; there I'll lead thee.
But be a man ; for thou'rt to mix with men
Fit to disturb the peace of all the world,
And rule it when 'tis wildest.
 Jaf. I give thee thanks
For this kind warning. Yes, I'll be a man ;
And charge thee, Pierre, whene'er thou see'st my fears
Betray me less, to rip this heart of mine
Out of my breast, and show it for a coward's.
Come, let's be gone, for from this hour I chase
All little thoughts, all tender human follies,
Out of my bosom : vengeance shall have room—
Revenge !   [*Going,* ¤
 Pierre. And liberty !
 Jaf. Revenge ! revenge !   [*Exeunt,* ¤

SCENE II.—*A Room in the House of Aquilina.*

Enter RENAULT, L. S. E.

 Ren. (c.) Why was my choice ambition ? The worst
  ground
A wretch can build on ! 'tis, indeed, at distance,
A goodly prospect, tempting to the view ;
The height delights us, and the mountain top
Looks beautiful, because 'tis nigh to heaven ;
But we ne'er think how sandy's the foundation,
What storm will batter, and what tempest shake us.
Who's there ?

Enter SPINOSA, L.

 Spin. (L. C.) Renault, good morrow, for by this time,
I think, the scale of night has turned the balance,
And weighs up morning. Has the clock struck twelve ?
 Ren. (R.) Yes ; clocks will go as they are set : but man
Irregular man's ne'er constant, never certain.
I've spent at least three precious hours of darkness
In waiting dull attendance ; 'tis the curse
Of diligent virtue to be mixed, like mine,

With giddy tempers, souls but half resolved.
Spin. (L.) Hell seize that soul amongst us it can fright-
en!
Ren. (c.) What's then the cause that I am here alone?
Why are we not together?

Enter ELLIOT, L.

Oh, sir, welcome!
You are an Englishman: when treason's hatching,
One might have thought you'd not have been behind hand.
Elliot. Frenchman, you are saucy.
Ren. (L. C.) How?   [*Puts his hand to his sword.*

Enter BEDAMAR, MEZZANA, DURAND, *and* THEODORE, L.—
Mezzana, Durand, and Theodore stand back, L.

Beda. [*Crossing,* c.] At difference? fie!
Is this a time for quarrels? Thieves and rogues
Fall out and brawl: should men of your high calling,
Men, separated by the choice of Providence
From the gross heap of mankind, and set here
In this assembly, as in one great jewel,
T' adorn the bravest purpose it e'er smiled on;
Should you, like boys, wrangle for trifles?
Ren. (R. C.) Boys!
Beda. (C.) Renault, thy hand.
Ren. I thought I'd given my heart,
Long since, to every man that mingles here;
But grieve to find it trusted with such tempers,
That can't forgive my froward age its weakness.
Beda. Elliot, thou once hadst virtue. I have seen
Thy stubborn temper bend with godlike goodness,
Not half thus courted. 'Tis thy nation's glory
To hug the foe that offers brave alliance.
Once more, embrace, my friends—
United thus, we are the mighty engine,
Must twist this rooted empire from its basis.
Totters it not already?
Elliot. (L.) 'Would 'twere tumbling!
Beda. Nay, it shall down: this night we seal its ruin.

Enter PIERRE, L. D.

Ah, Pierre! thou art welcome.

Come to my breast ; for, by its hopes, thou look'st
Lovelily dreadful ; and the fate of Venice
Seems on thy sword already. Oh, my Mars '
The poets that first feigned a god of war,
Surely prophesied of thee !
    Pierre. (l.) Friends, was not Brutus
(I mean that Brutus, who, in open senate,
Stabbed the first Cæsar that usurped the world),
A gallant man ?
    Ren. (r. c.) Yes, and Catiline too ;
Though story wrong his fame ; for he conspired
To prop the reeling glory of his country ı
His cause was good.
    Beda. (l. c.) And ours as much above it,
As, Renault, thou'rt superior to Cethegus,
Or Pierre to Cassius.
    Pierre. Then to what we aim at!
When do we start ?   Or must we talk forever ?
    Beda. (c.) No, Pierre, the deed's near birth : fate seems
        to have set
The business up, and given it to our care ;
I hope there's not a heart or hand amongst us,
But what is firm and ready.
    Elliot. (l. c.) All.
We'll die with Bedamar.
    Beda. Oh, men,
Matchless, as will your glory be hereafter :
The game is for a matchless prize, if won ;
If lost, disgraceful ruin.
    Pierre. Ten thousand men are arméd at your nod,
Commanded all by leaders fit to guide
A battle for the freedom of the world :
This wretched state has starved them in its service ;
And, by your bounty quickened, they're resolved
To serve your glory, and revenge their own :
They've all their different quarters in this city,
Watch for the alarm, and grumble 'tis so tardy.
    Beda. I doubt not, friend, but thy unwearied diligence
Has still kept waking, and it shall have ease ;
After this night, it is resolved, we meet
No more, till Venice owns us for her lords.
    Pierre. How lovelily the Adriatic, then,

Dressed in her flames, will shine ! Devouring flames !
Such as shall burn her to the watery bottom,
And hiss in her foundation !
   Beda. Now, if any
Amongst us here, that own this glorious cause,
Have friends or int'rest he would wish to save,
Let it be told—the general doom is sealed ;
But I'd forego the hopes of a world's empire,
Rather than wound the bowels of my friend.
   Pierre. I must confess, you there have touched my
      weakness.
I have a friend—hear it ; and such a friend !
My heart was ne'er shut to him. Nay, I'll tell you.
He knows the very business of this hour ;   [*All start*
But he rejoices in the cause, and loves it :
We've changed a vow to live and die together,
And he's at hand, to ratify it here.
   Ren. How ! all betrayed !
   Pierre. (c.) No ; I've dealt nobly with you.
I've brought my all into the public stock :
I'd but one friend, and him I'll share amongst you :
Receive, and cherish him ; or if, when seen
And searched, you find him worthless—as my tongue
Has lodged this secret in his faithful breast,
To ease your fears, I wear a dagger here,
Shall rip it out again, and give you rest,
Come forth, thou only good I e'er could boast of.

   Enter JAFFIER, *with a Dagger in his hand,* L. D.

   Beda. (c.) His presence bears the show of manly vir-
      tue !
   Jaf. (L.) I know you'll wonder all, that, thus uncalled
I dare approach this place of fatal councils ;
But I'm amongst you, and, by Heaven, it glads me
To see so many virtues thus united
To restore justice, and dethrone oppression.
Command this steel, if you would have it quiet,
Into this breast ; but, if you think it worthy
To cut the throats of reverend rogues in robes,
Send me into the cursed assembled Senate :
It shrinks not, though I meet a father there.
Would you behold the city flaming ? here's

A hand, shall bear a lighted torch at noon
To th' arsenal, and set its gates on fire !
Ren. (c.) You talk this well, sir.
Jaf. Nay, by Heaven, I'll do this !
Come, come, I read distrust in all your faces;
You fear me villain, and, indeed, 'tis odd
To hear a stranger talk thus, at first meeting,
Of matters that have been so well debated :
But I come ripe with wrongs, as you with counsels.
I hate this senate—am a foe to Venice ;
A friend to none but men resolved like me
To push on mischief. Oh, did you but know me,
I need not talk thus !
Beda. Pierre, I must embrace him ;
My heart beats to this man, as if it knew him.
Ren. I never loved these huggers.
Jaf. Still, I see
The cause delights me not. Your friends survey me,
As I were dangerous. But I come armed
Against all doubts, and to your trusts will give
A pledge, worth more than all the world can pay for.
My Belvidera ! Hoa ! my Belvidera !   [*Calls at* L. ●
Beda. (L. c.) What wonder next ?
Jaf. Let me entreat you, sirs,
As I have henceforth hope to call you friends,
That all but the ambassador, and this
Grave guide of councils, with my friend, that owns me,
Withdraw awhile, to spare a woman's blushes.
          [*Exeunt all but Bedamar, Renault, Jaffier, and Pierre,
          who stand back on* L.
Beda. Pierre, whither will this ceremony lead us ?
Jaf. My Belvidera ! Belvidera !   [*Calling*
Bel. [*Within,* L. D.] Who,
Who calls so loud, at this late peaceful hour ?
That voice was wont to come in gentle whispers,
And fill my ears with the soft breath of love.

          Enter BELVIDERA, L. D.

Thou hourly image of my thoughts, where art thou ?
Jaf. Indeed, 'tis late.
Bel. Alas ! where am I ? whither is't you lead me ?
Methinks I read distraction in your face,—

You shake and tremble, too! your blood runs cold!
Heav'ns guard my love, and bless his heart with patience !
Jaf. That I have patience, let our fate bear witness,
                                           [*Join hands.*
Who has ordained it so, that thou and I,
(Thou, the divinest good man e'er possessed,
And I, the wretched'st of the race of man,)
This very hour, without one tear, must part.
   Bel. Part! must we part ? Oh! am I then forsaken !
Why drag you from me ? [*Drawing to the* R.] whither are
       you going?
My dear! my life! my love!
   Jaf. (c.) Oh, friends !   [*To Renault,* &c.
   Bel. (c.) Speak to me !   [*To Jaffier*
   Jaf. Take her from my heart,
She'll gain such hold else, I shall ne'er get loose.
I charge you, take her, but with tenderest care
Relieve her troubles and assuage her sorrows.
                            [*She leans on Jaffier.*
   Ren. [*Advancing to her.*] Rise, madam, and command
       among your servants—
   Jaf. To you, sirs, and your honours, I bequeath her,
                            [*They lay hold of her*
And with her, this ; whene'er I prove unworthy—
                            [*Gives a Dagger to Renault.*
You know the rest—Then strike it to her heart ;
And tell her, he, who three whole happy years,
Lay in her arms, and each kind night repeated
The passionate vows of still increasing love,
Sent that reward, for all her truth and sufferings.
   Bel. [*Held between Bed. & Ren.*] Oh, thou unkind one !
Have I deserved this from you ?
Look on me, tell me, speak, thou dear deceiver,
Why am I separated from thy love ?
If I am false, accuse me ; but if true,
Don't, pr'ythee don't, in poverty forsake me,
                            [*Breaks away, and runs back to Jaffier*
But pity the sad heart, that's torn with parting.
                            [*They retake her*
Yet, hear me ; yet, recall me. Jaffier, Jaffier !
   [*Exeunt Bedamar, &c., dragging her* L. S. E., *Jaffier* R.
                   END OF ACT II.
       C

ACT III.

Scene I.—*A Room in the House of Aquilina.*

Enter BELVIDERA, L. S. E.

Bel. I'm sacrificed! I'm sold—betrayed to shame!
Inevitable ruin has enclosed me!
He, that should guard my virtue, has betrayed it;—
Left me—undone me! Oh, that I could hate him!—
Where shall I go? Oh, whither, whither wander?

Enter JAFFIER, R.

Jaf. (R. C.) Can Belvidera want a resting-place,
When these poor arms are open to receive her?
There was a time—
Bel. (C.) Yes, yes, there was a time
When Belvidera's tears, her cries and sorrows,
Were not despised; when, if she chanced to sigh,
Or look but sad——There was, indeed, a time,
When Jaffier would have ta'en her in his arms,
Eased her declining head upon his breast,
And never left her, till he found the cause.
But well I know why you forsake me thus;
I am no longer fit to bear a share
In your concernments: my weak female virtue
Must not be trusted: 'tis too frail and tender. [*Crosses*, R.
Jaf. Oh, Portia, Portia, what a soul was thine!
Bel. [*Returns to* L. C.] That Portia was a woman; and
      when Brutus,
Big with the fate of Rome (Heav'n guard thy safety!)
Concealed from her the labours of his mind,
She let him see her blood was great as his,
Flowed from a spring as noble, and a heart
Fit to partake his troubles, as his love.
Fetch, fetch that dagger back, the dreadful dower
Thou gav'st last night, in parting with me; strike it
Here to my heart; and as the blood flows from it,
Judge if it run not pure as Cato's daughter's.
Jaf. (R.) Oh, Belvidera!
Bel. (C.) Why was I last night delivered to a villain?

Jaf. Ha! a villain?

Bel. (R.] Yes, to a villain! Why, at such an hour,
Meets that assembly, all made up of wretches,
That look as hell had drawn them into league?
Why, I in this hand, and in that, a dagger,
Was I delivered with such dreadful ceremonies?
" To you, sirs, and your honours, I bequeath her,
And with her, this: Whene'er I prove unworthy—
You know the rest—then strike it to her heart."
Oh! [*Turns from him.*] why's that rest concealed from
        me?   Must I
Be made the hostage of a hellish trust?
For such, I know I am; that's all my value.
But, by the love and loyalty I owe thee,
I'll free thee from the bondage of these slaves!
Straight to the senate—tell them all I know,   [*Going,* L
All that I think, all that my fears inform me.

Jaf. (c.) Is this the Roman virtue? this the blood,
That boasts its purity with Cato's daughter?
Would she have e'er betrayed her Brutus? [*Going to her*

Bel. (L.) No;
For Brutus trusted her. [*Leans on him.*] Wert thou so
        kind,
What would not Belvidera suffer for thee?

Jaf. I shall undo myself, and tell thee all—
Yet think a little, ere thou tempt me further;
Think I've a tale to tell will shake thy nature,
Melt all this boasted constancy thou talk'st of,
Into vile tears and despicable sorrows;
Then, if thou shouldst betray me—

Bel. Shall I swear?

Jaf. No, do not swear: I would not violate
Thy tender nature with so rude a bond;
But, as thou hop'st to see me live my days,
And love thee long, lock this within thy breast:
I've bound myself, by all the strictest sacraments,
Divine and human—

Bel. Speak!

Jaf. To kill thy father—

Bel. My father! [*Part.*]

Jaf. Nay, the throats of the whole senate
Shall bleed, my Belvidera. He, amongst us,

That spares his father, brother, or his friend,
Is damned.
   Bel. Oh!
   Jaf. Have a care, and shrink not even in thought
For, if thou dost—
   Bel. (L. c.) I know it : thou wilt kill me.
Do! strike thy sword into this bosom : lay me
Dead on the earth, and then thou wilt be safe.
Murder my father! Though his cruel nature,
Has persecuted me to my undoing,
Driven me to basest wants ; can I behold him,
With smiles of vengeance, butchered in his age !
The sacred fountain of my life destroyed ?
And canst thou shed the blood that gave me being ?
                [*Leans on him*
Nay, be a traitor, too, and sell thy country!
Can thy great heart descend so vilely low,
Mix with hired slaves, bravos, and common stabbers,
Join such a crew, and take a ruffian's wages,
To cut the throats of wretches as they sleep ?   [*Part.*
   Jaf. (R. c.) Thou wrong'st me, Belvidera! I've en-
      gaged
With men of souls, fit to reform the ills
Of all mankind : there's not a heart among them,
But's stout as death, yet honest as the nature
Of man first made, ere fraud and vice were fashion.
   Bel. (L.) What's he, to whose cursed hands last night
      thou gav'st me ?
Was that well done ? Oh! I could tell a story,
Would rouse thy lion heart out of its den,
And make it rage with terrifying fury !
   Jaf. (c.) Speak on, I charge thee!
   Bel. Oh, my love! [*Leaning on him,*] if e'er
Thy Belvidera's peace deserved thy care,
Remove me from this place. Last night! last night!
   Jaf. Distract me not, but give me all the truth !
   Bel. No sooner wert thou gone, and I alone,
Left in the power of that old son of mischief;
No sooner was I laid on my sad bed,
But that vile wretch approached me. Then my heart
Throbbed with its fears ;—
Oh, how I wept and sighed,

And shrunk, and trembled ! wished, in vain, for nim
That should protect me ! Thou, alas, wast gone !
  Jaf. [*Turning,* R.] Patience, sweet Heaven, till I make
vengeance sure !
  Bel. He drew the hideous dagger forth, thou gav'st him,
And, with upbraiding smiles, he said, " Behold it :
This is the pledge of a false husband's love :"
And in his arms then pressed, and would have clasped
      me ;
But, with my cries, I scared his coward heart,
Till he withdrew, and muttered vows to hell.
                      [*Rush into each other's arms.*
These are thy friends ! [*Part.*] with these thy life, thy ho-
      nour,
Thy love, all staked—and all will go to ruin !
  Jaf. (c,) No more; I charge thee, keep this secret
      close.
Clear up thy sorrows ; look as if thy wrongs
Were all forgot, and treat him like a friend,
As no complaint were made. No more ; retire,
Retire, my life, and doubt not of my honour ;
I'll heal its failings, and deserve thy love.
  Bel. (L.) Oh ! should I part with thee, I fear thou wilt
In anger leave me, and return no more.
  Jaf. Return no more ! I would not live without thee
Another night, to purchase the creation.
  Bel. When shall we meet again ?
  Jaf. Anon, at twelve,
I'll steal myself to thy expecting arms :
Come, like a travelled dove, and bring thee peace.
  Bel. Indeed !
  Jaf. By all our loves !
  Bel. 'Tis hard to part :
But sure no falsehood ever looked so fairly.
Farewell ! remember twelve.   [*Exit,* L. B
  Jaf. (c.) Let Heav'n forget me,
When I remember not thy truth, thy love !

              Enter PIERRE, R.

  Pierre. Jaffier !
  Jaf. (L.) Who calls ?
  Pierre. (R. c.) A friend, that could have wished

T' have found thee otherwise employed.   What, hunt
A wife, on the dull soil !   Sure, a stanch husband,
Of all hounds is the dullest.   Wilt thou never,
Never be weaned from caudles and confections ?
What feminine tales hast thou been list'ning to,
Of unaired shirts ? catarrhs, and tooth-ache, got
By thin-soled shoes ?   Damnation ! tna: a fellow,
Chosen to be a sharer in the destruction
Of a whole people, should sneak thus in corners,
To waste his time, and fool his mind with love !
   Jaf. (L. c.) May not a man, then, trifle out an hour
With a kind woman, and not wrong his calling ?
   Pierre. (R.) Not in a cause like ours.
   Jaf. Then, friend, our cause
Is in a damned condition : for I'll tell thee,
That canker-worm, called lechery, has touched it ;
'Tis tainted vilely.   Wouldst thou think it ?   Renault,
(That mortified, old, withered, winter rogue,)
Loves simple fornication like a priest ;
I've found him out at watering for my wife ;
He visited her last night, like a kind guardian ;
Faith, she has some tempations, that's the truth on't.
   Pierre. (R. c.) He durst not wrong his trust !
   Jaf. 'Twas something late, though,
To take the freedom of a lady's chamber.
   " *Pierre.* Was she in bed ?
   " *Jaf.* Yes, 'faith ! in virgin sheets,
   " White as her bosom, Pierre ; dished neatly up,—
   " Might tempt a weaker appetite to taste."
   Pierre. Patience guide me !
He used no violence ?
   Jaf. No, no : out on't, violence !
Played with her neck ; brushed her with his grey beard ;
Struggled and touzed ; tickled her till she squeaked a lit-
    tle,
May be, or so—but not a jot of violence—
   Pierre. [*Runs to* R. D.] Damn him !
   Jaf. Ay, so say I : but, hush, no more on't !
Sure it is near the hour
We all should meet for our concluding orders :
Will the ambassador be here in person ?
   Pierre. (R. c.) No, he has sent commission to that villain,

Renault, to give the executing charge :
I'd have thee be a man, if possible,
And keep thy temper : for a brave revenge
Ne'er comes too late.
    Jaf. (c.) Fear not; I'm cool as patience;
    Pierre. He's yonder, coming this way, through the hall :
His thoughts seem full.
    Jaf. Pr'ythee, retire, and leave me
With him alone; I'll put him to some trial ;
See how his rotten part will bear the touching.
    Pierre. Be careful, then.
    Jaf. Nay, never doubt, but trust me.
                              [*Exit Pierre,* R. U. E.
What! be a devil, take a damning oath
For shedding native blood ?   Can there be sin,
In merciful repentance ?   Oh, this villain ! [*Retires up,* C

                Enter RENAULT, L. U. E.

    Ren. (L. C.) Perverse and peevish : What a slave is
        man,
To let his itching flesh thus get the better of him !
Despatch the tool, her husband—that were well.—
Who's there ?
    Jaf. A man.   [*Advancing*
    Ren. My friend, my near ally,
The hostage of your faith, my beauteous charge, is very
        well.
    Jaf. (R. C.) Sir, are you sure of that ?
Stands she in perfect health ?   Beats her pulse even ?
Neither too hot nor cold ?
    Ren. What means that question ?
    Jaf. Oh ! women have fantastic constitutions,
Inconstant in their wishes, always wavering,
And never fixed.   Was it not boldly done,
Ev'n at first sight, to trust the thing I loved
(A tempting treasure, too,) with youth so fierce
And vigorous as thine ? but thou art honest.
    Ren. Who dares accuse me ?
    Jaf. Cursed be he that doubts
Thy virtue !   I have tried it, and declare,
Were I to choose a guardian of my honour,
I'd put it in thy keeping ; for I know thee.

Ren. Know me!
Jaf. Ay, know thee.—There's no falsehood in thee;
Thou look's just as thou art.   Let us embrace.—
Now, wouldst thou cut my throat, or I cut thine!
Ren. You dare not do't!
Jaf. You lie, sir!
Ren. How!   •
Jaf. No more.—
'Tis a base world, and must reform; that's all.

Enter SPINOSA, ELLIOT, THEODORE, DURAND, *and* MEZZA-
NA, L.

Ren. Spinosa, Theodorè, you are welcome.
Spin. You are trembling, sir.
Ren. 'Tis a cold night, indeed; and I am aged;
Full of decay, and natural infirmities.
We shall be warm, my friends, I hope, to-morrow.
            [*Renault and Conspirators retire and confer.*

Enter PIERRE, R.

Pierre. |*To Jaffier.*] 'Twas not well done; thou shouldst
    have stroked him,
And not have galled him.   [*Retires to the others*
Jaf. (c.) [*In front.*] Damn him, let him chew on't!
Heav'n! where am I? beset with cursèd fiends,
That wait to damn me!   What a devil's man,
When he forgets his nature!—hush, my heart.
            [*Renault and the Conspirators advance*
Ren. My friends, 'tis late: are we assembled all?
Spin. All—all!
Ren. (c.) Oh! you're men, I find,
Fit to behold your fate, and meet her summons.
To-morrow's rising sun must see you all
Decked in your honours.   Are the soldiers ready?
Pierre. All—all!
Ren. You, Durand, with your thousand, must possess
St. Mark's; you, Captain, know your charge already;
'Tis to secure the ducal palace: •
Be all this done with the least tumult possible,
Till in each place you post sufficient guards;
Then sheathe your swords in every breast you meet.

Jaf. (L.) [*Aside.*] Oh, reverend cruelty! damned, bloody
villain !

Ren. During this execution, Durand, you
Must in the midst keep your battalia fast :
And, Theodore, be sure to plant the cannon
That may command the streets ;
This done, we'll give the general alarm,
Apply petards, and force the ars'nal gates ;
Then fire the city round in several places,
Or with our cannon, if it dare resist,
Batter to ruin. But, above all, I charge you,
Shed blood enough ; spare neither sex nor age,
Name nor condition : if there lives a senator
After to-morrow, though the dullest rogue
That e'er said nothing, we have lost our ends.
If possible, let's kill the very name
Of senator, and bury it in blood.

Jaf. [*Aside to* R.) Merciless, horrid slave !   Ay, blood
enough !
Shed blood enough, old Renault ! how thou charm'st me !

Ren. But one thing more, and then farewell, till fate
Join us again, or sep'rate us forever :
But let us all remember,
We wear no common cause upon our swords :
Let each man think, that on his single virtue,
Depends the good and fame of all the rest ;
Eternal honour, or perpetual infamy.
You droop, sir.   [*To Jaffier.*

Jaf. (L. C.) No : with most profound attention
I've heard it all, and wonder at thy virtue.

Ren. Let's consider,
That we destroy oppression—avarice ;
A people nursed up equally with vices
And loathsome lusts, which nature most abhors,
And such as, without shame, she cannot suffer.

Jaf. (L.) [*Aside,*] Oh, Belvidera ! take me to thy arms,
And show me where's my peace, for I have lost it.
                                        [*Exit,* L. D.

Ren. (L. C.) Without the least remorse, then, let's re-
solve
With fire and sword t'exterminate these tyrants,
Under whose weight this wretched country labours.

Pierre. (R.) And may those Powers above, that are pro-
pitious
To gallant minds, record this cause, and bless it!
Ren. (L.) Thus happy, thus secure of all we wish for,
Should there, my friends, be found among us one
False to this glorious enterprise, what fate,
What vengeance, were enough for such a villain?
Elliot. (R. C.) Death here, without repentance—hell
hereafter!
Ren. (C.) Let that be my lot, if, as here I stand,
Listed by fate among her darling sons,
Tho' I had one only brother, dear by all
The strictest ties of nature,
Joined in this cause, and had but ground to fear
He meant foul play; may this right hand drop from me,
If I'd not hazard all my future peace,
And stab him to the heart before you! Who,
Who would do less? Would'st thou not, Pierre, the same?
Pierre. You've singled me, sir, out for this hard ques-
tion,
As if 'twere started only for my sake:
Am I the thing you fear? Here, here's my bosom;
Search it with all your swords. Am I a traitor?
Ren. No: but I fear your late commended friend
Is little less. Come, sirs, 'tis now no time
To trifle with our safety. Where's this Jaffier?
Spin. (R. C.) He left the room just now, in strange dis-
order.
Ren. Nay, there is danger in him: I observed him;
During the time I took for explanation,
He was transported from most deep attention
To a confusion, which he could not smother.
What's requisite for safety, must be done
With speedy execution; he remains
Yet in our power; I, for my own part, wear
A dagger—
Pierre. Well?   [*Goes to Renault*
Ren. And I could wish it—
Pierre. Where?   .
Ren. Buried in his heart.
Pierre. Away! we're yet all friends.—
No more of this; 'twill breed ill blood among us.

Spin. Let us all draw our swords, and search the house ;
Pull him from the dark hole, where he sits brooding
O'er his cold fears, and each man kill his share of him.
     Pierre. (L.) Who talks of killing ?   Who's he'll shed
          the blood,
That's dear to me ?   I'st you, or you, or you, sir ?
                         [*Passing from* L. *to* R.
What ! not one speak ? how you stand gaping all
On your grave oracle, your wooden god there !
Yet not a word ?   Then, sir, I'll tell you a secret ;
Suspicion's but at best a coward's virtue.   [*To Renault.*
     Ren. (c.) A coward !   [*Handles his sword.*
     Pierre. (R.) Put—Put up thy sword, old man ;
Thy hand shakes at it.   Come, let's heal this breach ;
I am too hot : we yet may all live friends.
     Spin. Till we are safe, our friendship cannot be so.
     Pierre. Again !   Who's that ?
     Spin. 'Twas I.
     Theo. And I.
     Ren. And I.
     Spin. And all.
Let's die like men, and not be sold like slaves.
     Pierre. (c.) One such word more, by Heaven, I'll to the
          senate,
And hang ye all, like dogs, in clusters.
Why peep your coward swords half out their sheaths ?
Why do you not all brandish them like mine ?
You fear to die, and yet dare talk of killing.   [*Going,* L
     Ren. (R. c.) Go to the senate, and betray us—haste !
Secure thy wretched life ; we fear to die
Less than thou dar'st be honest.
     Pierre. That's rank falsehood.
Fear'st thou not death ?   Fie, there's a knavish itch
In that salt blood, an utter foe to smarting !
Had Jaffier's wife proved kind, he'd still been true.
Faugh—how that stinks !   [*Exit Renault,* R.
" Thou die ? thou kill my friend ?
" Or thou ? with that lean, withered, wretched face !"
Away, disperse all to your several charges,
And meet to-morrow, where your honour calls you,
                         [*Retiring to* M. D
I'll bring that man whose blood you so much thirst for.

And you shall see him venture for you fairly——
Hence, hence, I say!
Spin. I fear we've been to blame,
And done too much.
Theo. 'Twas too far urged against the man you love
Elliot. Forgive us, gallant friend.
Pierre. [*Advancing.*] Nay, now you've found
The way to melt, and cast me as you will.
I 'll fetch this friend, and give him to your mercy;
Nay, he shall die, if you will take him from me;
For your repose, I'll quit my heart's best jewel;
But would not have him torn away by villains,
And spiteful villainy.
Spin. [*And other Conspirators stand,* n.] No; may ye
both
Forever live, and fill the world with fame!
Pierre. Now, you're too kind. Whence arose all this
discord?
Oh! what a dangerous precipice have we 'scaped!
How near a fall was all we'd long been building!
What an eternal blot had stained our glories,
If one, the bravest and the best of men,
Had fall'n a sacrifice to rash suspicion,
Butchered by those, whose cause he came to cherish!
Oh, could you know him all, as I have known him,
How good he is, how just, how true, how brave,
You would not leave this place, till you had seen him,
And gained remission for the worst of follies.
Come but to-morrow, all your doubts shall end,
And to your loves, me better recommend,
That I've preserved your fame, and saved my friend.
[*Exeunt Conspirators,* R., *Pierre* L

END OF ACT III.

ACT IV.

Scene I.—*A Street.*

Enter Belvidera *and* Jaffier, l.

Jaf. (l. c.) Where dost thou lead me ? Ev'ry step I
move,
Methinks I tread upon some mangled limb
Of a racked friend. Oh, my dear, charming ruin !
Where are we wandering ?
  Bel. (r. c.) To eternal honour !
To do a deed, shall chronicle thy name
Among the glorious legends of those few
That have saved sinking nations. Every street
Shall be adorned with statues to thy honour :
And, at thy feet, this great inscription written—
" Remember him, that propped the fall of Venice !"
  Jaf. Rather, remember him, who, after all
The sacred bonds of oaths, and holier friendship,
In fond compassion to a woman's tears,
Forgot his manhood, virtue, truth, and honour,
To sacrifice the bosom that relieved him.
Why wilt thou damn me ?
  Bel. Oh, inconstant man !
How will you promise ! how will you deceive !
Do, return back, replace me in my bondage,
Tell all thy friends how dangerously thou lov'st me,
And let thy dagger do its bloody office.
Or, if thou think'st it nobler, let me live,
Till I'm a victim to the hateful will
Of that infernal devil !
Last night, my love—
  Jaf. Name, name it not again :
Destruction, swift destruction,
Fall on my coward head, if
I forgive him !
  Bel. Delay no longer, then, but to the senate,
And tell the dismal'st story ever uttered ;
Tell them what bloodshed, rapines, desolations,
Have been prepared ;—how near's the fatal hour.

D

Save thy poor country, save the rev'rend blood
Of all its nobles, which to-morrow's dawn
Must else see shed!
    Jaf. Oh!
    Bel. Think what then may prove
My lot : the ravisher may then come safe,
And, 'midst the terror of the public ruin,
Do a damned deed.
    Jaf. By all Heav'n's powers, prophetic truth dwells in
        thee!
For every word thou speak'st, strikes through my heart,
Like a new light, and shows it how't has wandered—
Just what thou'st made me, take me, Belvidera,
And lead me to the place, where I'm to say
This bitter lesson ; where I must betray
My truth, my virtue, constancy, and friends.
Must I betray my friends ?   Ah ! take me quickly,
Secure me well before that thought's renewed ;
If I relapse once more, all's lost forever.
    Bel. Hast thou a friend more dear than Belvidera?
    Jaf. No : Thou'rt my soul itself; wealth, friendship,
        honour!
All present joys, and earnest of all future,
Are summed in thee.   [*Going,* n.

    Enter CAPTAIN *and* GUARDS, R. S. E.

    Capt. Stand! who goes there?
    Bel. Friends.
    Capt. But what friends are you ?
    Bel. Friends to the senate, and the state of Venice.
    Capt. My orders are, to seize on all I find
At this late hour, and bring them to the council,
Who are now sitting.
    Jaf. Sir, you shall be obeyed.
Now the lot's cast, and, fate, do what thou wilt.
        [*Exeunt Jaffier and Belvidera, guarded.*

    SCENE II.—*The Senate House.*

The DUKE OF VENICE, PRIULI, *and other* SENATORS *disco-
        vered, sitting.*

    Duke. Antony, Priuli, senators of Venice,

Speak—Why are we assembled here this night !
What have you to inform us of, concerns
The state of Venice' honour, or its safety ?
  Priuli. (R.) Could words express the story I've tc tell
    you,
Fathers, these tears were useless, these sad tears
That fall from my old eyes ; but there is cause
We all should weep, tear off these purple robes,
And wrap ourselves, in sackcloth, sitting down
  On the sad earth, and cry aloud to heaven :
Heav'n knows, if yet there be an hour to come, ·
Ere Venice be no more.
  Duke. How !
  Priuli. Nay, we stand   .
Upon the very brink of gaping ruin.
Within this city's formed a dark conspiracy
To massacre us all, our wives and children,
Kindred and friends ; our palaces and temples
To lay in ashes : nay, the hour, too, fixed ;
The swords, for aught I know, drawn ev'n this moment,
And the wild waste begun. From unknown hands
I had this warning : but, if we are men,
Let's not be tamely butchered, but do something
That may inform the world in after ages,
Our virtue was not ruined, though we were.
                    [*A noise within,* L.
  Capt. [*Within.*] Room, room, make room there for some
    prisoners !

                Enter OFFICER, L.

  Duke. Speak, speak, there !   What disturbance ?
  Officer. A prisoner have the guards seized in the street,
Who says, he comes to inform this reverend council
About the present danger.

    Enter OFFICER, JAFFIER, CAPTAIN, *and* GUARDS, L.

  All. Give him entrance.—[*Exit Officer.*] Well, who are
    you ?
  Jaf. (L.) A villain !   ·
Would, every man that hears me,
Would deal so honestly, and own his title !
  Duke. 'Tis rumored, that a plot has been contrived

Against the state, and you've a share in't, too.
If you're a villain, to redeem your honour,
Unfold the truth, and be restored with mercy.
   Jaf. Think not, that I to save my life came hither;
I know its value better; but in pity
To all those wretches, whose unhappy dooms
Are fixed and sealed. You see me here before you,
The sworn and covenanted foe of Venice :
But use me as my dealings may deserve,
And I may prove a friend.
   Duke. The slave capitulates ;
Give him the tortures.
   Jaf. That, you dare not do :
Your fears won't let you, nor the longing itch
To hear a story, which you dread the truth of:
Truth, which the fear of smart shall ne'er get from me.
Cowards are scared with threat'nings ; boys are whipped
Into confessions : but a steady mind
Acts of itself, ne'er asks the body counsel.
Give him the tortures !—name but such a thing
Again, by heav'n, I'll shut these lips forever !
Nor all your racks, your engines, or your wheels,
Shall force a groan away, that you may guess at !
                                [*Crosses,* ₌
   Duke. Name your conditions.
   Jaf. (ᴿ.) For myself, full pardon,
Besides, the lives of two-and-twenty friends,
Whose names I have enrolled—Nay, let their crimes
Be ne'er so monstrous, I must have the oaths,
And sacred promise, of this reverend council,
That, in a full assembly of the senate,
The thing I ask be ratified. Swear this,
And I'll unfold the secrets of your danger.
   Duke. Propose the oath.
   Jaf. (ᴄ.) By all the hopes
You have of peace and happiness hereafter,
Swear !
   Duke. We swear.
   Jaf. And, as ye keep the oath,
May you and your posterity be blessed,
Or cursed, forever !
   Duke. Else be cursed forever

Jaf. Then here's the list, and with't, the full disclosure
·[*Delivers two papers to the Officer, who delivers them to
the Duke.*
Of all that threaten you.
Now, Fate, thou hast caught me!
Duke. Give order, that all diligent search be made
To seize these men—their characters are public.
The paper intimates their rendezvous
To be at the house of the famed Grecian courtesan,
Called Aquilina; see that place secured.
You, Jaffier, must with patience bear till morning
To be our prisoner.·
Jaf. ·Would the chains of death
Had bound me fast, ere I had known this minute!
Duke. Captain, withdraw your prisoner.
Jaf. Sir, [*To Officer,*] if possible,
Lead me where my own thoughts themselves may lose
me ;
Where I may doze out, what I've left of life ;—
Forget myself, and this day's guilt and falsehood.
Cruel remembrance ! how shall I appease thee ?
       •   [*Exit, guarded,* R
Officer. [*Without.*] More traitors ! room, room, room,
make room there !
Duke. How's this ?
The treason's
'Already at the doors !

      Enter OFFICER *and* CAPTAIN, L.

Officer. My lords, more traitors !
Seized in the very act of consultation :
Furnished with arms and instruments of mischief.—
Bring in the prisoners !

  Enter SPINOSA, ELLIOT, THEODORE, DURAND, MEZZANA,
    RENAULT, *and* PIERRE, *in Chains,* L.

Pierre. (L.) You, my lords and fathers,
(As you are pleased to call yourselves,) of Venice ;
If you set here to guide the course of justice,
Why these disgraceful chains upon the limbs
That have so often laboured in your service ?

Are these the wreaths of triumph you bestow
On those that bring you conquest home, and honours ?
Duke. Go on! you shall be heard; sir.
Pierre. (L. C.) Are these the trophies I've deserved for
    fighting
Your battles with confederated powers ?
When winds and seas conspired to overthrow you,
And brought the fleets of Spain to your own harbours,
When you, great duke, shrunk trembling in your palace ;
Stepped not I forth, and taught your loose Venetians
The task of honour, and the way to greatness ?
Raised you from your capitulating fears
To stipulate the terms of sued-for peace ?
And this my recompence ! If I'm a traitor,
Produce my charge ; or show the wretch that's base,
And brave enough to tell me, I'm a traitor !
                          [*Goes to the table.*
  Duke. Know you one Jaffier ?
  Pierre. Yes, and know his virtue.
His justice, truth, his general worth, and sufferings
From a hard father, taught me first to love him.
  Duke. See him brought forth.

     Enter CAPTAIN, *with* JAFFIER *in Chains,* R.

  Pierre. My friend, too, bound! nay, then,
Our fate has conquered us, and we must fall.
Why droops the man, whose welfare's so much mine,
They're but one thing ? These reverend tyrants, Jaffier
Do call us traitors. Art thou one, my brother ?
  Jaf. (R. C.) To thee I am the falsest, veriest slave.
That e'er betrayed a generous, trusting friend,
And gave up honour to be sure of ruin.
All our fair hopes, which morning was to've crowned,
Has this cursed tongue o'erthrown.
  Pierre. (C.) So, then, all's over :
Venice has lost her freedom, I my life.
No more !   [*Crosses,* L
  Duke. Say ; will you make confession
Of your vile deeds, and trust the senate's mercy ?
  Pierre. [*Returns to* C.] Cursed be your senate, cursed
    your constitution!
The curse of growing factions, and divisions,

Still vex your councils, shake your public safety,
And make the robes of government you wear
Hateful to you, as these base chains to me!
Duke. Pardon, or death ?
Pierre. Death! honourable death!
Ren. (L.) Death's the best thing we ask, or you can
      give.
Duke. Break up the council. Captain, guard your pri-
      soners.
Jaffier, you're free ; but theee must wait for judgment.
      [*Exeunt Duke, Senators, Conspirators, and Officer.* ,
Pierre. (c.) Come, where's my dungeon ? Lead me to
      my straw :
It will not be the first time I've lodged hard,
To do your senate service.
Jaf. (R. C.) Hold, one moment.
Pierre. Who's he disputes the judgment of the senate ?
Presumptuous rebel !—on—   [*Strikes Jaffier*
Jaf. (c.) By Heaven, you stir not !   .
                        [*Exeunt Captain and Guards,* R.
I must be heard ! I must have leave to speak.
Thou hast disgraced me, Pierre, by a vile, blow :
Had not a dagger done thee nobler justice ?
But use me as thou wilt, thou can'st not wrong me,
For I am fallen beneath the basest injuries ;
Yet look upon me with an eye of mercy,   ,
And, as there dwells a godlike nature in thee,
Listen with mildness to my supplications.
      Pierre. (R. C.) What whining monk art thou ? what ho-
      ly cheat,
That would'st encroach upon my credulous ears,
And cant'st thus vilely ! Hence ! I know thee not !
Jaf. Not know me, Pierre !
Pierre. No, know thee not. What art thou ?
Jaf. Jaffier, thy friend, thy once loved, valued friend !
Tho' now deservedly scorned, and used most hardly.
      Pierre. Thou, Jaffier ! thou, my once-loved, vaued
      friend !
By heavens, thou ly'st ; the man so called my friend,
Was generous, honest, faithful, just, and valiant ;
Noble in mind, and in his person lovely ;
Dear to my eyes, and tender to my heart :

But, thou, a wretched, base, false, worthless coward,
Poor, even in soul, and loathsome in thy aspect :
All eyes must shun thee, and all hearts detest thee.
Pr'ythee, avoid, nor longer cling thus round me,
Like something baneful, that my nature's chilled at.
   Jaf. I have not wronged thee ; by these tears I have
     not !
   Pierre. Hast thou not wronged me ?   Dar'st thou call
     thyself
That once-loved, honest, valued friend of mine,
And swear thou hast not wronged me ?   Whence these
     chains ?
Whence the vile death which I may meet this moment ?
Whence this dishonour, but from thee, thou false one ?
   Jaf. All's true ; yet grant one thing, and I've done ask
     ing.
   Pierre. What's that ?
   Jaf. To take thy life, on such conditions
The council have proposed : thou, and thy friends,
May yet live long, and to be better treated.
   Pierre. Life ! ask my life ! confess ! record myself
A villain, for the privilege to breathe,
And carry up and down this cursèd city,
A discontented and repining spirit,
Burdensome to itself, a few years longer !
· To lose it, may be, at last, in a lewd quarrel
For some new friend, treacherous and false as thou art !
No, this vile world and I have long been jangling,
And cannot part on better terms than now,
When only men like thee art fit to live in't.
   Jaf. By all that's just—
   Pierre. Swear by some other power,
For thou hast broke that sacred oath too lately.
   Jaf. Then by that hell I merit, I'll not leave thee
Till, to thyself at least, thou'rt reconciled,
However thy resentments deal with me. ·
   Pierre. Not leave me !
   Jaf. No ; thou shalt not force me from thee.
Use me reproachfully, and like a slave ;
Tread on me, buffet me, heap wrongs on wrongs
On my poor head ; I'll bear it all with patience,
Shall weary out thy most unfriendly cruelty :

Lie at thy feet, [*Falls on his knees,*] and kiss them tho'
 they spurn me ;
Till, wounded by my sufferings, thou relent,
And raise me to thy arms with dear forgiveness.
' *Pierre.* Art thou not—
 Jaf. What ?
 Pierre. A traitor ?
 Jaf. Yes.
 Pierre. A villain ?
 Jaf. Granted.
 Pierre. A coward, a most scandalous coward ; .
Spiritless, void of honour ; one who has sold
Thy everlasting fame, for shameless life ?
 Jaf. [*Rising and turning,* R.] All, all, and more, much
 more ; my faults are numberless.
 Pierre. And would'st thou have me live on terms like
 thine ?
Base, as thou'rt false—
 Jaf. [*Returning.*] No ; 'tis to me that's granted ;
The safety of thy life was all I aimed at,
In recompence for faith and trust so broken.
 Pierre. I scorn it more, because preserved by thee ;
And, as when first my foolish heart took pity
On thy misfortunes, sought thee in thy miseries,
Relieved thy wants, and raised thee from the state
Of wretchedness, in which thy fate had plunged thee,
To rank thee in my list of noble friends ;
All I received in surety for thy truth,
Were unregarded oaths, and this, this dagger,
Given with a worthless pledge, thou since hast stol'n :
So I restore it back to thee again ;
Swearing by all those powers which thou hast violated,
Never from this cursed hour, to hold communion,
Friendship, or interest, with thee, though our years
Were to exceed those limited the world.
Take it—farewell—for now I owe thee nothing
 Jaf. Say thou wilt live, then.
 Pierre. For my life, dispose it
Just as thou wilt, because 'tis what I'm tired with.
 Jaf Oh. Pierre !
 Pierre. No more.   [*Going,* a
 Jaf. My eyes won't lose the sight of thee, [*Following*

But languish after thine, and ache with gazing.
 Pierre. Leave me—Nay, then, thus, thus I throw thee
    from me ;
And curses, great as is thy falsehood, catch thee !
                    [*Drives him to* c.—*Exit,* ʀ.
 Jaf. [*Pausing.*] He's gone, my father, friend, preserver ।
And here's the portion he has left me :
This dagger.   Well remembered ! with this dagger
I gave a solemn vow of dire importance ;
Parted with this, and Belvidera together.
, Have a care, mem'ry, drive that thought no farther ·
No, I'll esteem it as a friend's last legacy ;
Treasure it up within this wretched bosom,
Where it may grow acquainted with my heart,
That, when they meet, they start not from each other.
So, now for thinking—A blow—called traitor, villain,
Coward, dishonourable coward ; faugh !
Oh, for a long, sound sleep, and so forget it !
Down, busy devil !

              Enter BELVIDERA, ʟ.

 Bel. (ʟ.) Whither shall I fly ?
Where hide me and my miseries together ?
Where's now the Roman constancy I boasted ?
Sunk into trembling fears and desperation,
Not daring to look up to that dear face,
Which used to smile, even on my faults : but, down,
Bending these miserable eyes to earth,
Must move in penance, and implore much mercy.
 Jaf. (ʀ. c.) Mercy ! kind Heaven has surely endless
    stores
Hoarded for thee, of blessings yet untasted :
" Let wretches loaded hard with guilt as I am,
" Bow with the weight, and groan beneath the burden,
" Before the footstool of that Heav'n they've injured."
Oh, Belvidera ! I'm the wretched'st creature
E'er crawled on earth.
 Bel. (ʟ. c.) Alas ! I know thy sorrows are most mighty
 Jaf. My friend, too, Belvidera, that dear friend,
Who, next to thee, was all my heart rejoiced in,
Has used me like a slave, shamefully used me :
'Twould break thy pitying heart to hear the story

Bel. What has he done?

Jaf. " Oh, my dear angel! in that friend, I've lost
' All my soul's peace; for every thought of him
" Strikes my sense hard, and deads it in my brain!
' Would'st thou believe it?
" Before we parted,"
Ere yet his guards had led him to his prison,
Full of severest sorrows for his sufferings,
As at his feet I kneeled, and sued for mercy,
With a reproachful hand he dashed a blow :
He struck me, Belvidera! by Heaven, he struck me
Buffeted, called me traitor, villain, coward!
Am I a coward? am I a villain? tell me :
Thou'rt the best judge, and mad'st me, if I am so!
Damnation! coward!

Bel. Oh! forgive him, Jaffier!
And, if his sufferings wound thy heart already,
What will they do to-morrow?

Jaf. Ah!

Bel. To-morrow,
When thou shalt see him stretched in all the agories
Of a tormenting and a shameful death;
What will thy heart do then? Oh! sure 'twill stream,
Like my eyes now.

Jaf. What means thy dreadful story?
Death, and to-morrow?

Bel. (c.) The faithless senators, 'tis they've decreed it,
They say, according to our friends' request,
They shall have death, and not ignoble bondage ;
Declare their promised mercy all as forfeited :
False to their oaths, and deaf to intercession,
Warrants are passed for public death to-morrow.

Jaf. Death! doomed to die! condemned unheard! un
pleaded!

Bel. Nay, cruel'st racks and torments are preparing
To force confession from their dying pangs.
Oh! do not look so terribly upon me!
How your lips shake, and all your face disordered!
What means my love?

Jaf. Leave me, I charge thee, leave me! Strong temp
tations
Wake in my heart.

Bel. (L.) For what?
Jaf. No more, but leave me.
Bel. Why?
Jaf. (L. C.) Oh! by Heav'n, I love thee with that fond-
ness,
I would not have thee stay a moment longer
Near these cursed hands.
[*Pulls the Dagger half out of his bosom, and puts it
back again.*
Art thou not terrified?
Bel. No.
Jaf. Call to mind
What thou hast done, and whither thou hast brought me.
Bel. Ha!
Jaf. Where's my friend? my friend, thou smiling mis-
chief!
Nay, shrink not, now 'tis too late; for dire revenge
Is up, and raging for my friend.   He groans!
Hark, how he groans! his screams are in my ears!
Already, see, they've fixed him on the wheel,
And now they tear him—Murder! perjured senate!
Murder—Oh! Hark thee, traitress, thou hast done this!
Thanks to thy tears, and false persuading love.
How her eyes speak! oh, thou bewitching creature!
Madness can't hurt thee.   Come, thou little trembler,
Creep even into my heart, and there lie safe;
'Tis thy own citadel—Hah—yet stand off,   [*Going,* R
Heav'n must have justice, and my broken vows
Will sink 'me else beneath its reaching mercy.
I'll wink, and then 'tis done—
Bel. (C.) What means the lord
Of me, my life, and love?   What's in thy bosom
Thou grasp'st at so?
[*Jaffier draws the Dagger, and offers to stab her*
Ah! do not kill me, Jaffier.
Jaf. (R. C.) Know, Belvidera, when we parted last,
I gave this dagger with thee, as in trust,
To be thy portion if I e'er proved false.
On such condition was my truth believed:
But now 'tis forfeited, and must be paid for.
[*Offers to stab her again.*
Bel. Oh! mercy!

Jaf. Nay, no struggling.
Bel. Now, then, kill me.
                 [Falls on his neck, and kisses him
While thus I cling about thy cruel neck,
Kiss thy revengeful lips, and die in joys
Greater than any I can guess hereafter.   ·
   Jaf. I am, I am a coward, witness, Heav'n,
Witness it, earth, and ev'ry being witness :
'Tis but one blow ! yet, by immortal love,
I cannot longer bear the thought to harm thee.
           [Throws away the dagger, and embraces her
The seal of Providence is sure upon thee ;
And thou wast born for yet unheard-of wonders.
Oh ! thou wert born either to save or damn me !
By all the power that's given thee o'er my soul,
By thy resistless tears and conquering smiles,
" By the victorious love that still waits on thee,"
Fly to thy cruel father, save my friend,
Or all our future quiet's lost forever.
Fall at his feet, cling round his rev'rend knees,
Speak to him with thy eyes, and with thy tears,
Melt his hard heart, and wake dead nature in him,
Nor, till thy prayers are granted, set him free,
But conquer him, as thou hast vanquished me.
               [Exeunt Jaffier, R., *Belvidera,* L

END OF ACT IV.

———◆———

ACT V.

SCENE I.—*An Apartment in Priuli's House.*

Enter PRIULI, L.

   Priuli. (L.) Why, cruel Heav'n, have my unhappy days
Been lengthened to this sad one ? Oh ! dishonour,
And deathless infamy have fall'n upon me.
Was it my fault ? Am I a traitor ? No. (C.)
But then, my only child, my daughter wedded ;

There my best blood runs foul, and a disease
Incurable has seized upon my memory.

Enter BELVIDERA *in a Mourning Veil,* L.

Bel. [*Speaking as she enters.*] He's there, my father, n y
inhuman father,
That, for three years, has left an only child,
Exposed to all the outrages of fate,
And cruel ruin !—Oh !—
Priuli. What child of sorrow
Art thou, that com'st, wrapt up in weeds of sadness,
And mov'st as if thy steps were towards a grave ?
Bel. (L. C.) A wretch, who, from the very top of happi-
ness,
Am fallen into the lowest depths of misery,
And want your pitying hand to raise me up again.
Priuli. (R. C.) What wouldst thou beg for ?
Bel. Pity and forgiveness.   [*Throws up her Veil.*
By the kind, tender names of child and father,
Hear my complaints, and take me to your love.   [*Kneels.*
Priuli. My daughter !
Bel. Yes, your daughter ; and you've oft told me,
With smiles of love, and chaste paternal kisses,
I'd much resemblance of my mother.
Priuli. Don't talk thus.
Bel. Yes, I must : and you must hear, too.
I have a husband.
Priuli. Damn him !
Bel. Oh, do not curse him !
He would not speak so hard a word towards y.u,
On any terms, howe'er he deal with me.
Priuli. Ah ! what means my child ?
Bel. Oh ! my husband, my dear husband,
Carries a dagger in his once kind bosom,
To pierce the heart of your poor Belvidera !
Priuli. Kill thee !
Bel. Yes, kill me. When he passed his faith
And covenant against your state and senate,
He gave me up a hostage for his truth :
With me a dagger, and a dire commission,
Whene'er he failed, to plunge it through this bosom
I learnt the danger, chose the hour of love

T' attempt his heart, and bring it back to honour.
Great love prevailed, and blessed me with success!
He came, confessed, betrayed his dearest friends,
For promised mercy. Now, they're doomed to suffer!
Galled with remembrance of what then was sworn,
If they are lost, he vows t' appease the gods
With this poor life, and make my blood th' atonement.
    Priuli. Heavens!
    Bel. If I was ever then your care, now hear me!
Fly to the senate, save the promised lives
Of his dear friends, ere mine be made the sacrifice.
    Priuli. Oh, my heart's comfort!
    Bel. Will you not, my father?
Weep not, but answer me.
    Priuli. By Heav'n, I will!
Not one of them but what shall be immortal!
Canst thou forgive me all my follies past?
I'll henceforth be indeed a father! never,
Never more, thus expose, but cherish thee,
Dear as the vital warmth that feeds my life:
Dear as these eyes, that weep in fondness o'er thee;
Peace to thy heart. Farewell!
    Bel. Go, and remember,
'Tis Belvidera's life her father pleads for!
                          [*Exeunt Priuli,* R., *Belvidera,* L

SCENE II.—*The Rialto.*

Enter CAPTAIN—*Muffled Drums*—GUARDS—EXECUTIONER
with Axe—RENAULT—SPINOSA—ELLIOT—THEODORE—
DURAND—-MEZZANA——PIERRE—OFFICER—-GUARDS—
They all pass over the Stage, R. *to* L., *and exeunt.*

SCENE III.—*A Street.*

Enter JAFFIER, R.

Jaf. Final destruction seize on all the world!
Bend down, ye Heav'ns, and, shutting round this earth
Crush the vile globe into its first confusion!

Enter BELVIDERA, L.

Bel. (c.) My life!—

Jaf. (R. c.) My plague!—
Bel. Nry, then, I see my ruin.
If I must die!
Jaf. (c.) No, death's this day too busy;
Thy father's ill-timed mercy came too late.
I thank thee for thy labours, though; and him too.
But all my poor, betrayed, unhappy friends,
Have summons to prepare for fate's black hour.
Yet, Belvidera, do not fear my cruelty,
Nor let the thoughts of death perplex thy fancy :
But answer me to what I shall demand,
With a firm temper and unshaken spirit.
Bel. (L. c.) I will, when I've done weeping—
Jaf. Fie, no more on't!
How long is't since the miserable day
We wedded first ?
Bel. Oh! oh!
Jaf. Nay, keep in thy tears,
Lest they unman me quite.
Bel. Heaven knows I cannot!
The words you utter sound so very sadly,
The streams will follow—
Jaf. Come, I'll kiss them dry, then.
Bel. [*Hanging on him.*] But was't a miserable day ?
Jaf. A cursed one!
Bel. I thought it otherwise, and you've often sworn,
When sure you spoke the truth, you've sworn you blessed
it.
Jaf. 'Twas a rash oath.
Bel. Then why am I not cursed, too ?
Jaf. No, Belvidera; by th' eternal truth,
I dote with too much fondness.
Bel. Still so kind!
Still then do you love me ?
Jaf. Man ne'er was blessed,
Since the first pair first met, as I have been.
Bel Then sure you will not curse me ?
Jaf. No, I'll bless thee.
I came on purpose, Belvidera, to bless thee.
'Tis now, I think, three years we've lived together.
Bel. And may no fatal minute ever part us,
Till, reverend grown, for age and love, we go

Down to one grave, as our last bed together ;
There sleep in peace till an eternal morning.
Jaf. Did I not say I came to bless thee ?
Bel. You did.   *Part*
Jaf. Then hear me, bounteous Heaven !   [*Knieling*
Pour down your blessings on this beauteous head,
Where everlasting sweets are always springing, .
With a continual giving hand : let peace,
Honour, and safety, always hover round her :
Feed her with plenty ; let her eyes ne'er see
A sight of sorrow, nor her heart know mourning ;
Crown all her days with joy, her.nights with rest,
Harmless as her own thoughts ; and prop her virtue
To bear the loss of one that too much loved ;
And comfort her with patience in our parting?
Bel. How ? parting, parting !
Jaf. Yes, forever parting !
I have sworn, Belvidera, by yon Heav'n,
That best can tell how much I lose to leave thee,
We part this hour forever !
Bel. Oh ! call back
Your cruel blessing ; stay with me, and curse me.
Jaf. Now hold, heart, or never !
Bel. By all the tender days we've lived together,
Pity my sad condition ; speak, but speak !
Jaf. Murder ! unhold me ;
Or by th' immortal destiny that doomed me
                                  [*Draws his dagger.*
To this cursed minute, I'll not live one longer !
Resolve to let me go, or see me fall—
Hark ! the dismal bell   [*Passing bell tolls.*
Tolls out for death !   I must attend its call, too ;
For my poor friend, my dying Pierre, expects me ;
He sent a message to require I'd see him
Before he died, and take his last forgiveness.
Farewell forever !   [*Going, L.*
Bel. Leave thy dagger with me ;
Bequeath me something—Not one kiss at parting !
Oh, my poor heart, when wilt thou break ?
Jaf. [*Returning—she runs into his arms.*] Yet stay :
We have a child, as yet a tender infant :
Be a kind mother to him when I'm gone ;

Breed him in virtue and the paths of honour,
But never let him know his father's story !
I charge thee, guard him from the wrongs my fate
May do his future fortune or his name.
Now—nearer yet—
Oh, that my arms were riveted
Thus round thee ever !   But my friends ! my oath !
This, and no more !   [*Kisses her*
    Bel. Another, sure another
For that poor little one you've ta'en such care of.
I'll give't him truly.
    Jaf. So—now, farewell !
    Bel. Forever ?   [*Going,* L.
    Jaf. Heav'n knows, forever ! all good angels guard
        thee !   [*Exit,* L
    Bel. All ill ones, sure, had charge of me this moment !
Oh, give me daggers, daggers, [*Returns,* C.] fire, or water !
How I could bleed, how burn, how drown, the waves
Huzzing and foaming round my sinking head,
Till I descended to the peaceful bottom !
Oh ! there's all quiet—here, all rage and fury !
The air's too thin, and pierces my weak brain ;
I long for thick substantial sleep : (R. C.) Hell ! hell !
Burst from the centre, (R.) rage and roar aloud,
If thou art half so hot, so mad as I am !   [*Exit,* R

SCENE IV.—*St. Mark's Place.*—*A Scaffold in the back
    ground, and a Wheel, prepared for the Execution of
    Pierre.*

Enter CAPTAIN, PIERRE, GUARD, EXECUTIONER, *and* RAB-
                    BLE.

Pierre. (L.) My friend not yet come ?

            Enter JAFFIER, R.

Jaf. Oh, Pierre !   [*Falling on his knees*
Pierre. (C.) Dear to my arms, though thou'st undone
    my fame,
I can't forget to love thee. Pr'ythee, Jaffier,
Forgive that filthy blow, my passion dealt thee :
I'm now preparing for the land of peace

And fain would have the charitable wishes
Of all good men like thee, to bless my journey.
   Jaf. Good ! I'm the vilest creature—worse than e'er
Suffered the shameful fate thou'rt going to taste of.
   Capt. (R.) The time grows short; your friends are dead
     already.
   Jaf. (L. C.) Dead !
   Pierre. Yes, dead, Jaffier ! they've all died like men,
     too,
Worthy their character.
   Jaf. And what must I do ?
   Pierre. Oh, Jaffier !
   Jaf. Speak aloud thy burdened soul,
And tell thy troubles to thy tortured friend.
   Pierre. Friend ! Couldst thou yet be a friend, a gene-
     rous friend,
I might hope comfort from thy noble sorrows.
Heaven knows, I want a friend !
   Jaf. And I a kind one,
That would not scorn thus my repenting virtue,
Or think, when he's to die, my thoughts are idle.
   Pierre. No ! live, I charge thee, Jaffier.
   Jaf. Yes, I will live :
But it shall be to see thy fall revenged,
At such a rate, as Venice long shall groan for
   Pierre. Wilt thou ?
   Jaf. I will, by Heaven !
   Pierre. Then still thou'rt noble,
And I forgive thee. Oh !—yet—shall I trust thee ?
   Jaf. No ; I've been false already.
   Pierre. Dost thou love me ?
   Jaf. Rip up my heart, and satisfy thy doubtings.
   Pierre. Curse on this weakness !   [*Weeps.*
   Jaf. Tears ! Amazement ! Tears !
I never saw thee melted thus before ;
And know there's something labouring in thy bosom,
That must have vent; though I'm a villain, tell me.
   Pierre. See'st thou that engine ? [*Pointing to the Wheel.*
   Jaf. Why ?
   Pierre. (R. C.) Is't fit a soldier, who has lived with honor,
Fought nations' quarrels, and been crowned with con-
     quest,

Be exposed, a common carcase, on a wheel ?
Jaf. Hah !
Pierre. Speak ! is't fitting ?
Jaf. Fitting !
Pierre. I'd have thee undertake
Something that's noble, to preserve my memory
From the disgrace that's ready to attaint it.
    Capt. The day grows late, sir.
    Pierre. I'll make haste. Oh, Jaffier !
Though thou'st betrayed me, do me some way justice.
    Jaf. What's to be done ?
    Pierre. This and no more.   [*Whispers Jaffier.*
    Jaf. Hah ! is't then so ?
    Pierre. Most certainly.
    Jaf. I'll do't.
    Pierre. Remember.
    Capt. Sir—
    Pierre. Come, now I'm ready.
Captain, [*Crossing to him*] you should be a gentleman of
    honour ;
Keep off the rabble, that I may have room
To entertain my fate, and die with decency.
You'll think on't ?   [*To Jaffier.*
    Jaf. 'Twont grow stale before to-morrow.
    [*Pierre and Jaffier ascend the Scaffold—Executioner
    binds Pierre.*
    Pierre. Now, Jaffier ! now I'm going ! Now—
    Jaf. Have at thee,
Thou honest heart, then !—here—   [*Stabs him.*
And this is well, too.   [*Stabs himself.*
    Pierre. Now, now—thou hast indeed been faithful !
This was done nobly !—We've deceived the senate.
    Jaf. Bravely !
    Pierre. Ha ! ha ! ha !—oh ! oh !
    [*Falls down on the Scaffold and dies*
    Jaf. Now, ye cursed rulers,
Thus of the blood ye've shed, I make libation,
And sprinkle it mingling. May it rest upon you.
And all your race ! Oh, poor Belvidera !
Sir, I've a wife ; bear this in safety to her,
A token that, with my dying breath, I blessed her,

And the dear little infant left behind me.
I'm sick—I'm quiet.   [*Dies.—The Scene shuts upon them.*

SCENE V.—*An Apartment in Priuli's House.*

Enter PRIULI, R.; BELVIDERA, *distracted; and two of her Women.*

Priuli. (L. c.) Strengthen her heart with patience, pity-
   ing Heav'n !
Bel. (c.) Come, come, come, come, come ; nay, come to
   bed,
Pr'ythee, my love.   The winds ! hark how they whistle !
And the rain beats !   Oh, how the weather shrinks me !
I say you shall not go, indeed you shall not :
Whip your ill-nature ; get you gone, then ; Oh !
Are you returned ?   See, father, here he's come again !
Am I to blame to love him ?   Oh, thou dear one !
Why do you fly me ?   Are you angry still, then ?
Jaffier, where art thou ?   Father, why do you do thus ?
Stand off ! don't hide him from me !   He's there some-
   where.
Stand off, I say !   What, gone ?   Remember, tyrant
I may revenge myself for this trick, one day.

Enter CAPTAIN OF THE GUARD, L., *and whispers Priuli.*

Priuli. News ! what news ?
Capt. (L.) Most sad, sir :
Jaffier, upon the scaffold, to prevent
A shameful death, stabbed Pierre, and next himself ;
Both fell together.
   Bel. (R.) Ha ! look there !
My husband bloody, and his friend, too !   Murder !
Who has done this ?   Speak to me, thou sad vision ;
On these poor trembling knees, I beg it.   Vanished :—
Here they went down. (R. c.)—Oh, I'll dig, dig the den
   up !
Hoa, Jaffier, Jaffier !
Peep up, and give me but a look.   I have him !
I have got him, father !   Oh !
My love ! my dear ! my b'essing ! help me ! help me !

They have hold of me, and drag me to the bottom !
Nay—now they pull so hard—farewell—   [*Dies, 3.*
 " *Priuli.* [*Bending over her*] Oh ! lead me to some place
    " that's fit for mourning ;
 " Where the free air, light, and the cheerful sun,
 " May never enter ; hang it round with black,
 " Set up one taper that may last a day,
 " As long as I've tc live ; and there all leave me :
 " Sparing no tears when you this tale relate,
 " But bid all cruel fathers dread my fate." [*Exeunt omnes*

DISPOSITION OF THE CHARACTERS AT THE FALL OF
                    THE CURTAIN.

MAIDS.   BELVIDERA AND PRIULI.   CAPTAIN.
R.]   [L.

CPSIA information can be obtained at www.ICGtesting.com
Printed in the USA
LVOW081720210613

339728LV00003B/358/P